Snug in the Tent

Written by Suzy Senior

Illustrated by Erin Brown

Collins

I like to camp in a tent.

It's best when it rains. I feel snug.

Now, there is just far too much rain.

Splish! Splash! Splosh!
Will this rain ever stop?

I see lots of droplets on the tent.

I hear them drip.

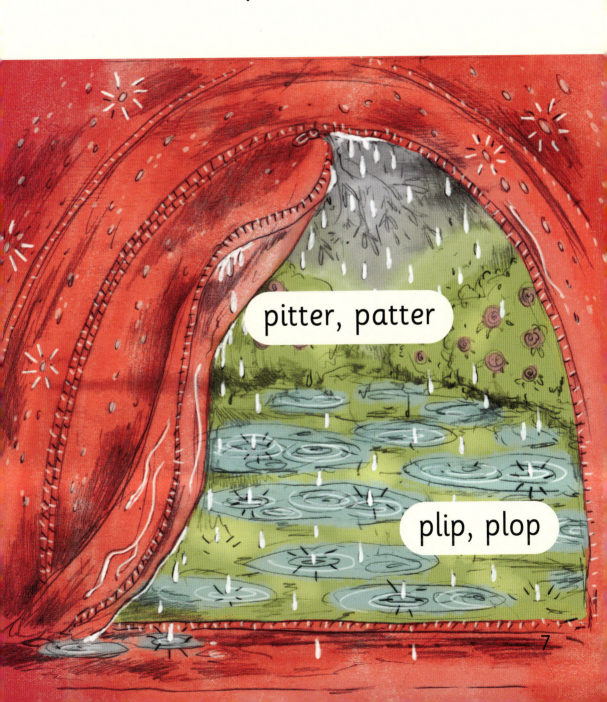

pitter, patter

plip, plop

Splat! Now the rain lands in the tent.

Drips splash into my rucksack.
My blanket gets damp.

Gran yells, "It's too wet for tents.
Come in!"

I grab my stuff and sprint back in.

I can still camp in my bedroom.

Yes, now I am snug in the tent!

What happens?

 Review: After reading

Use your assessment from hearing the children read to choose any GPCs, words or tricky words that need additional practice.

Read 1: Decoding

- Ask the children:
  - Can you think of any words that rhyme with **camp**? (e.g. *damp, ramp, lamp*) These words end in the adjacent consonants "m" "p".
  - Look through the book. What words can you find that begin with "s" "p" "l"? (*splat, splish, splash, splosh*)
  - Which of the following words rhyme with the word **best**? rest, stop, test, vest, bug, jest, tent, pest. (*rest, test, vest, jest, pest*) These words end in the adjacent consonants "s" "t".

Read 2: Prosody

- Model reading each page to the children with expression and voices to read the speech.
- Have fun reading the words **splish**, **splash**, **splosh** in different voices.
- After you have read each page, ask the children to have a go at reading with expression.

Read 3: Comprehension

- Turn to pages 14 and 15 and encourage the children to use the pictures to retell the story.
- For every question ask the children how they know the answer. Ask:
  - Look at page 9. What items get wet? (*rucksack and blanket*)
  - Why does Gran say it is time to come in? (*it is too wet for tents*)
  - What kind of tent would you make? What materials would you use?